# KENWORTH SEMI TRUCKS

Greg Smith
Photoillustrators

Captions by Kris Palmer

motorbooks

First published in 2009 by Motorbooks, an imprint of MBI Publishing Company, 400 First Avenue North, Suite 300, Minneapolis, MN 55401

Motorbooks titles are also available at discounts in bulk quantity for industrial or sales-promotional use. For details write to Special Sales Manager at MBI Publishing Company, 400 First Avenue North, Suite 300, Minneapolis, MN 55401 USA.

To find out more about our books, visit us online at www.motorbooks.com.

Library of Congress Cataloging-in-Publication Data

Smith, Greg
   Kenworth Semi Trucks/ Greg Smith
      p. cm.
   Includes index.
   ISBN-13: 978-0-7603-3394-5
   ISBN-10: 0-7603-3394-7
   1. Truck tractors—Customizing. 2. Tractor trailer combinations—Customizing. I. Title.
   TL230.5.T73G373 2006
   629.224—dc22
   2006019841

Editor: Tom Lund
Designer: Lindsay Haas

Printed in China

**Cover:**
Kenworth W900:
With a chopped top and sleeper, plus color-matched visor, this W900 looks long, low, and mean—in a good way. Note how chopping the top brings the windshield down, requiring a shortened wiper assembly. A little flourish with the custom silver paint blends a modern touch with this truck's classic lines to create a timeless look.

**Frontis:**
Kenworth K100:
Nothing beats the forward visibility of cabover. When you're maneuvering something as long as a tractor trailer, that can be handy, especially in tight quarters.

**Title Page:**
Kenworth 900L:
The 900 series is a great-looking truck. Add a few details like a metal bug deflector to the radiator surround, small visors to the headlights, and some custom lighting touches, and you have one beautiful hauler.

**Verso:**
*My Last Dream* 2001 Kenworth W900:
With a roomy Double Eagle sleeper and deep red finish, this rig is as easy on its owners, Judy and Jerry Reese, as it is on the eyes. If the road is your workplace, it's nice to have a rolling office like this one.

**Back Cover:**
*Inferno Joe* 1954 Kenworth:
This mean truck, *Inferno Joe*, actually combines body panels from the '54 with a more modern chassis from a '94 W900L. The result is traffic-stopping vintage body-lines and a pleasant, modern ride. These flames look so real, you'll want to hop into the cab quick to avoid the heat.

# Introduction

Photo illustration the Greg Smith way begins with a vehicle photographed under the best lighting conditions that time or setting permit. (Overcast days and soft light are ideal.) He prefers digital photographs because of their depth of detail and shoots at maximum resolution, pulling every detail the lens can find into the shot. Because he snaps many highly polished vehicles, he often shoots through a curtain to mask his own and other unwanted reflections.

From there, he imports the photograph into Photoshop software, and the illustration portion of this art's name kicks in. Smith loves to match vehicles to exciting, stimulating settings—places you'd love to visit or just gaze at for their beauty and remarkable features.

Though it's the product of love for photography, cars, and arresting imagery, Smith's art involves years of hard work too. At age 8 his father taught him film developing, and he's been fascinated with it ever since. He is the premier photo illustrator, with more than 28 years bringing great shots to grateful fans.

## *TOAD'S PAD*
## 2002 KENWORTH W900L

An orange-and-white paint scheme with gold accents provides a distinctive look to Tri-State Commodities' 2002 Kenworth W900L. Nicknamed *Toad's Pad*, this extreme truck makes a toad's life seem pretty good. Actually, it's Todd Stockman who is this machine's lucky driver. This Kenworth is a regular—and frequent winner—at truck shows.

## *INFERNO JOE*
# 1954 KENWORTH

Western Distributing bought this '54 Kenworth as a peer for their '53 Peterbilt—the company buys from both manufacturers. This mean truck, *Inferno Joe*, actually combines body panels from the '54 with a more modern chassis from a '94 W900L. The result is traffic-stopping vintage bodylines and a pleasant, modern ride. These flames look so real, you'll want to hop into the cab quick to avoid the heat.

## *NO FEAR*
## KENWORTH T600

Motorcycle fans will know clothing manufacturer No Fear. This tractor-trailer puts the No Fear logo on 18 wheels. The front end is all business and no glitter, which keeps onlookers' eyes on the rolling ad behind. Zipper motif and breakout logo stress the manufacturer's themes— clothing and rebellion. Menacing eyes atop the sleeper draw looks when the trailer is detached. Disk alloy wheels are understated but tough looking, like the Harley rims on the bike Arnold Schwarzenegger rides in *Terminator 2*.

## *TEQUILA SUNRISE*
## 2006 KENWORTH W900L

Truckers know well the blazing orange of the rising sun. This puller evokes the flaming horizon perfectly with a slow-fade paint job shifting from the bottom's dark orange to the light yellow on top of the cab and sleeper. Stylized flame accents along the side tie it all together, making this Kenworth as striking as the sunrise. Truck enthusiasts know this manufacturer even without the badge.

## *MEGUIAR'S CAR CRAZY* 2003 KENWORTH T2000

The mirror glaze on this truck was 100 years in the making. That's how long this family has been making polishes—initially for furniture and now, more than a century later, for surfaces of all sorts. Frank Meguiar Jr. began making polishes at his home with an eggbeater, one bottle at a time, in 1901. This is one idea that caught on big, and the company is still run by the Meguiar family. Shine on.

## *RAINBOW*
## 1974 KENWORTH W900A

Show stopper or show winner? Both. Sam Watson's '74 Kenworth W900A, known as *Rainbow*, took the Best of Show Bobtail award at the Stars & Stripes show in Las Vegas. Some nice touches on this truck include custom lighting along the bumper and around the lower portion of the cab and sleeper, with another set of lights along the sleeper's top line. Cab roof lights are echoed above the sleeper as well. Antennas boast of communications and entertainment features in this extreme truck.

# HAPPY HOUR
# 2002 KENWORTH
# W900L

Comfort on the road is important to sustaining the trucker lifestyle. This '02 Kenworth W900L has plenty of luxury to offer with its large aftermarket sleeper. Doug Day runs this rig for Hoosier Air Transport out of Columbus, Indiana. Think there's a hot tub in there? Tiki bar? With this rig's tinted windows, you'll just have to make friends with the owner to learn what's inside the *Happy Hour* truck.

## *HACIENDA MOTORCYCLES* KENWORTH W900

Motorcycles have a uniquely American feel, and so does this rig. Classic flames mark the hood and sleeper, with some smaller flames carried back to the trailer's corner and emerging behind a proud eagle. The nice thing about a trailer full of motorcycles is you

always have transportation. Hacienda Motorcycles has been serving the Safford, Arizona, area for more than 30 years. With this rig, they'll take bikes anywhere need requires.

## 2002 KENWORTH W900L

Rick Sladek's red W900L rides on a cushion of brightwork above polished bumper, wheels, steps, tanks, frame steps, and half fenders. Kenworth fender plates below the lights play off the polished visors, short and large, on the headlights and cab roof. We can't see into the sleeper here, but as an oft-shown machine, you can be sure it's comfy. Built in 2002, this truck shows how much of the classic look Kenworth has retained in its 900 series. How could you top a grille like that?

# 2003 KENWORTH W900L

Stylized silver flames lick the paint on this custom tractor. Wonder if the driver—whoa! Look at the spooky beast peering out of this sleeper, in paintwork of course. Gazing from a clawed hole is something sure to scare a few kids passing this truck. Half Grinch, half demonic clown, this paint detail has a look all its own. Think strangers disturb the driver at night with that face staring 'em down?

## 2004 KENWORTH W900L

*Covert* might be a good word for this badge-less rig's look. With no logos on the grille or hood and an even coat of orange paint, this extreme truck raises as many questions as it answers. The painted fenders on the tractor and trailer wrap around and obstruct part of the tire, carrying on this rig's mysterious ways. Even the trailer side is unlettered, leaving onlookers to decide what swiped a gash through the orange.

## 1993 KENWORTH W900L TANDEM DUMP TRUCK

When you need a hauler and you need it yellow, Corey and Hilary Wardlaw have you covered. This piggyback Reliance Transfer dump setup can haul a serious load—just what Kenworth tractors were designed to handle. But just because it's a work truck, doesn't mean it can't look as good as it hauls.

# 1982 KENWORTH W900

Diamond-plate steps and hefty angle-cut pipes add a touch of flash to this dark hauler. It belongs to Jeff England, who owns Pride Transport with his wife, Pat. Jeff likes a nice- looking truck so much, he co-founded the Great Salt Lake Truck Show. Great trucks are essential to Pride Transport and are sources of pride for their owners.

## *MY LAST DREAM*
## 2001 KENWORTH
## W900

With a roomy Double Eagle sleeper and deep red finish, this rig is as easy on its owners, Judy and Jerry Reese, as it is on the eyes. They got ideas for the truck's interior at truck shows. That dome on top of the sleeper is a TracStar satellite TV antenna, giving this Kenworth, *My Last Dream*, all the comforts of home. If the road is your workplace, it's nice to have a rolling office like this one.

# KENWORTH 900L

The 900 series is a great-looking truck. Add a few details like a metal bug deflector to the radiator surround, small visors to the headlights, and some custom lighting touches, and you have one beautiful hauler. Custom bumper with paired lights complements the dual headlights, while blue-lettered Bridgestones tie a routine item, tires, to this specific Kenworth for an integrated appearance throughout.

# 2000 KENWORTH T800 DUMP TRUCK

The term *purple people eaters* once described some linemen for the Minnesota Vikings. This rig is too big and too tough to take on people; it's designed for much rougher loads. The only problem with a truck this nice is that you don't want to scratch it. Dump trucks, especially Kenworths, aren't for the light stuff, though, so a couple of nicks just mean the truck is earning its keep.

# 1994 KENWORTH W900L

Erich Schoen runs this lowered Kenworth W900L with Western Trailers curtainsider. Schoen did a lot of the custom brightwork on this rig, which shows off the dark paint. These headlights have individual visors above each bulb, a nod to the precision with which this fine rig was built. A side pinstripe is subtle, breaking up the high, flat side panels and creating a sense of flow.

42

# KENWORTH W900

With a chopped top and sleeper plus color-matched visor, this W900 looks long, low, and mean—in a good way. Note how chopping the top brings the windshield down, requiring a shortened wiper assembly. A little flourish with the custom silver paint blends a modern touch with this truck's classic lines to create a timeless look.

# 2007 KENWORTH W900

Not too many tractors wear white, but this custom rig's lines, evocative of a 1930s sports car, need no pigment to make a statement. The custom front end has a vintage appeal, and the indents in the hood panel are reminiscent of louvers on some raw racing machine from eras past. Headlights repositioned to the bumper further reinforce the body-work's simple lines. Nameplates have been deleted to keep this Kenworth's look unique.

# 1977 KENWORTH W900L

If the sight of a moving van can be a little unsettling—a sign of big change—this Allied Van Lines rig should be reassuring. Any journey that starts with a hauler this nice can't be too bad. And operators who care enough to make their truck glimmer like new aren't going to set a cup of hot coffee on your Steinway. Customers who want to follow their precious cargo can see this rig's accessory lighting on the darkest nights.

# 1997 KENWORTH W900L

A little planning and style can go a long way. Red and white are basic vehicle colors that can go unnoticed in the wrong hands. This McLane Transport rig showcases simple bright red paint outlined in gold leaping out down the sides of the gleaming white tractor-trailer. Polished brightwork from front to back completes the look for one eye-grabbing extreme hauler.

## KENWORTH W900

Here's another take on color that pays off. Not too many vehicles feature medium and lighter shades of blue. Because little on the ground wears the shade, it really stands out, even below a blue boundless sky. If the muraled trailer looks show worthy, it should—Chevron Delo has sponsored truck shows like Overdrive's Pride & Polish. Auxiliary lights across the underside of the bumper add front-end variety after dark.

# *McK EXPRESS*
# 2005 KENWORTH W900L

Several custom touches call attention to
this fine hauler. Long lug-nut caps give a
Ben-Hur menace to the front wheels, while
horizontal bars set off the grille. Yellow
accents integrate the rig, from the fender
plates below the headlights to the striping
along the trailer's top and bottom edges.
Most catching about this extreme machine
is the skull in the McK Express logo.

# KENWORTH W900

While polished wheels are the standard among show trucks, this rig goes one step further with orange highlights. The fender plates pick up on the theme, as does the leading side of the cab steps. An understated pinstripe on the hood sides frames the Kenworth badge on a truck whose owner is obviously proud of his ride. Keeping that whole trailer polished to a shine is no enviable task, but it looks great.

# KENWORTH W900

Big ol' angled pipes suit this low roller well. Polished surfaces were carefully chosen to maintain a more classic look. Painted steps catch our attention while allowing polished bumper and fenders to stand out more than they would if everything at chassis level were plated and gleaming. This cab also looks chopped, lending more to the custom feel.

## KENWORTH T2000

Though no lettering proclaims its name, we can safely rule out a few monikers for this impressive rig—Big Blue, Black Knight, White Lightning. There are advantages to this scheme. One color of touch-up paint has you covered, and you can tell people you need to meet up with later to find you at the red truck. "Which one?," they might ask. "You'll know."

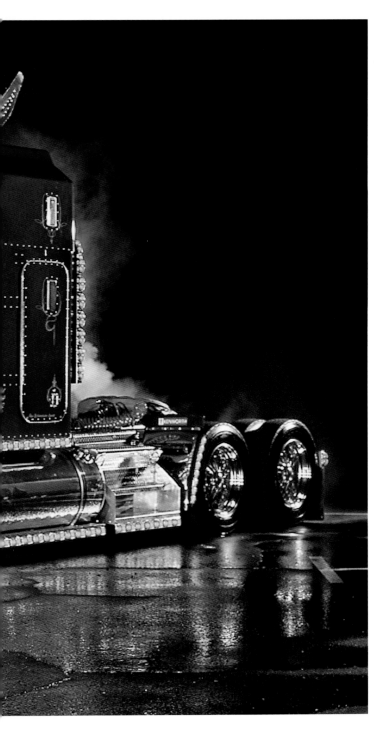

# KENWORTH W900

This fun truck looks like a toy, which may be why so many rigs are turned into toys for the young and young at heart. Of course, there's no goody-two-shoes here. This truck's for "bad" kids. Check out the pleated custom interior. The auxiliary lighting also looks great on this truck, thoughtfully placed toward the rear because the flames are the stars up front.

# KENWORTH T660

The T660 is one of Kenworth's aerodynamic designs and has been engineered for improved fuel economy. As this rig makes clear, a truck needn't be homely just because it does a little better at the pumps. This tractor still sports a characteristic Kenworth grille. While the cab roof features auxiliary lights, they sit low for minimal disruption of air currents. Stacks send the exhaust upward but not way upward, again providing less wind resistance.

# KENWORTH T2000

Sleek styling is what the T2000 is all about. Compared to most of the trucks in this book, which revel in their custom and polished componentry, the T2000 is about unity of design. The panels flow and merge, giving wind few protrusions or square faces to shove against. The bumper is integrated, the hood flows into the windshield, which flows into the sleeper, and all the chassis-height componentry blends together.

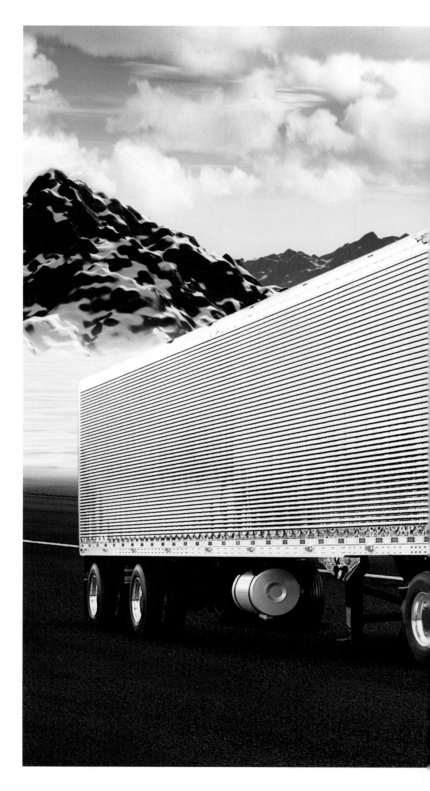

## *NY YANKEES* KENWORTH T2000

A tractor-trailer is not the best way for a whole baseball team to travel. No problem,
though, because this rig hauls a dragster, not ball players. George Steinbrenner got
involved with drag racing because his son, Hank, loves the sport. Steinbrenner teamed up

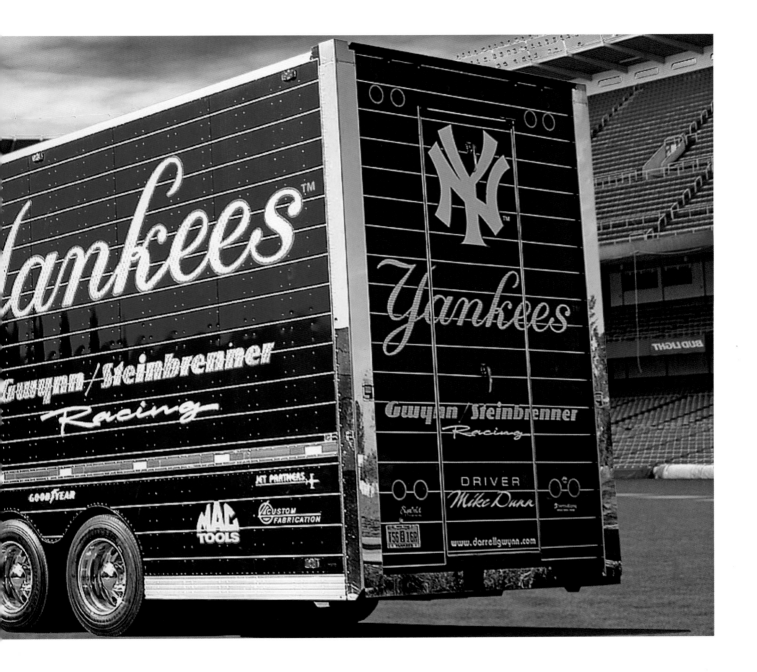

with another well-chosen celebrity, drag-racing legend Darrell Gwynn. Even though this rig serves racing, not baseball, the drivers still carry Yankees caps, which they give out between races.

# 2002 KENWORTH W900L

Dump trucks handle tough work, but they don't have to look beat up to prove it. Chris Schmidt's W900L has show-truck style with a paint-matched Raven rear-dump trailer. Even though the truck is plenty tough and built to work, you have to wonder if guys loading it take a little extra care with a rig this nice. Wouldn't you?

# 1997 KENWORTH T2000 RACE TRUCK

If the typical motorist's view of a truck is a rolling fortress to pass on the uphills and get passed by going down, this machine puts a whole new spin on truckin'.
Built for the drag strip with twin engines, this red racer can beat 100 miles per hour handily in the quarter. Another CFI truck that looks similar to this one set records at Bonneville with an out-and-back speed of more than 162 miles per hour.

## TRUK-RODZ
## 1996 KENWORTH
## W900L

Jones Performance Products began with Hap Jones's interest in racing in the late 1940s. He began working with fiberglass to save weight, and his passion for light, strong materials continued to grow, along with his knowledge and techniques for making parts with them. Today, son Dave runs the company, which makes fiberglass truck hoods in more than 80 styles. This race-themed tractor showcases some of the company's expertise.

# KENWORTH W900

Yellow works well for small vehicles. This truck proves that a powerful puller can wear it too. Color-matched tanks, fenders, and step sides bring it all together. Huge straight-cut stacks are always impressive, and this tractor is no exception.

# KENWORTH W900L

Purple isn't for every vehicle, but a Kenworth W900L wears it well. This rig also provides a good look at the differences between alloy and chrome goodies. The chrome bumper has a near-mirror finish, while the alloy front wheels shine but with a more opaque and silvery look. With gleaming flat chrome like this, you see what's reflected, while with alloy, you focus more on the shape of the piece itself.

## 1950s KENWORTH TANKER

It's a testament to Kenworth's build quality and the devotion of its fans that older trucks like this not only still run but look great and haul too. Horns and searchlights are matched on this tractor, although exhaust duties are handled with a single passenger-side stack. The finish on this truck stands up fine against the polished tanker.

# 1971 KENWORTH W923

This truck looks happy, and why not? Looks pretty good after 37 years of service. The fact that its owner cares is evident in more than clean paint and polished chrome. The cab step bears a boot scraper to keep that mud and grit off the floors. A covered grille suggests that this truck might see some cold weather too.

# 2001 KENWORTH W900 TANKER

When a combo setup slows you down on an incline, it may as well look good—and this one sure does. What a blend of polish and paint. The green accents on the tankers transform objects designed for pure practicality into stylish complements for a stout- looking tractor. Not many trucks making a delivery draw people out just to admire the rig, but this one no doubt does.

# 1932 KENWORTH STAKEBED

If you ever wondered about the early days, yep, Kenworths were tough then too. You could load a Model T truck onto the back of this one and go on your way without a struggle. While the grille badge is a little hard to make out, it features the stacked KW just as it appears today.

# KENWORTH W900

As owners of black vehicles will tell you, it's hard to keep them clean. It sure pays off when you do, though. An interesting touch to this tractor is that no orange lenses are visible. Instead, the lights use the tuner trick of white/clear lens and orange bulb for the same effect at night but a fresh look by day.

# KENWORTH
# BULLNOSE COMBO

The bullnose was a popular Kenworth in its day, and this one soldiers on in a combo rig, no less. Single searchlight, horn, and stack show less devotion to symmetry than modern tractors exhibit.

# KENWORTH K100

Nothing beats the forward visibility of a cabover. When you're maneuvering something as long as a tractor trailer, that can be handy, especially in tight quarters.

# KENWORTH T2000

Few people see as much of America as truckers do. This paint job celebrates the United States with the stars and stripes of Old Glory. The T2000's gracefully sculpted bodywork provides nice work surfaces for the custom painter. With the T2000's aerodynamics, the flag painting is the only thing flapping in the wind on this truck.

## KENWORTH W900

Many different changes can give a truck a unique look, as we've seen throughout this book. Chrome and auxiliary lighting are obvious favorites. Another way toward a distinctive look is to paint what is often polished, as this truck does well with orange and black.

# Index

Allied Van Lines, 46
Bridgestone, 36
CFI, 71
Chevron Delo, 51
Day, Doug, 20
Double Eagle, 35
England, Jeff, 32
Great Salt Lake Truck Show, 32
Gwynn, Darrell, 67
*Hacienda Motorcycles*, 22
*Happy Hour*, 20
Hoosier Air Transport, 20
*Inferno Joe*, 11
Jones Performance Products, 73
Kenworth models
    900L, 36
    Bullnose Combo, 88
    K100, 90
    Stakebed, 85
    T600, 12
    T660, 63
    T800 Dump Truck, 38
    Tanker, 79
    W900, 22, 32, 35, 43, 44, 51, 55, 56, 61, 75, 86, 94
    W900 Tanker, 82
    W900A, 19
    W900L, 8, 11, 15, 20, 25, 26, 29, 31, 41, 46, 48, 52, 68, 73, 77
    W900L Tandem Dump Truck, 31
    W923, 81
    T2000, 16, 59, 64, 67, 71, 92
    T2000 Race Truck, 71

*McK Express*, 52
McLane Transport, 48
Meguiar, Frank Jr., 16
*Meguiar's Car Crazy*, 16
*My Last Dream*, 35
*No Fear*, 12
*NY Yankees*, 67
Overdrive's Pride & Polish, 51
Peterbilt, 11
Pride Transport, 32
*Rainbow*, 19
Raven, 68
Reese, Judy and Jerry, 35
Reliance Transfer, 31
Schmidt, Chris, 68
Schoen, Erich, 41
Sladek, Rick, 25
Stars & Stripes show, Las Vegas, 19
Steinbrenner, George, 66
Stockman, Todd, 8
*Tequila Sunrise*, 15
*Toad's Pad*, 8
TracStar, 35
Tri-State Commodities, 8
*Truk-Rodz*, 73
Wardlaw, Corey and Hilary, 31
Watson, Sam, 19
Western Distributing, 11
Western Trailers, 41